The Way of The Clan

Thomas J. Mason

The Way of the Clan revised August 14, 2015

Revised December 8 2020

Cover design:

Thomas J. Mason

thomasjmason@att.net

ISBN: 9798578675379

Independently published

Table of Contents

Thomas J. Mason

ACKNOWLEDGEMENT

To Douglas Adams for "Life, the universe and everything" from "The Hitchhiker's Guide to the Galaxy" radio series and books.

To the Ancient Greeks for the trinity of "spirit, mind and body."

To the Ancient Indo-Europeans from India to Ireland for the concept of the three aspects of their Gods and their belief that the spirit animates the body and can live again in another body.

To the Hindus for the belief that there is a spark of the divine in each person.

To the unknown author of the "The Song of God," as the Indian poem, "The Bhagavad Gita" is known, for writing, "Thou and I have lived many lives."

To Orson Scott Card, for "Xenocide, book three in his "Ender" series, in which he uses the word, "aiua", which he took from the Sanskrit for "life", to describe non-material beings who can be pulled out of their own other-universe to animate bodies in this universe.

To Jesus of Nazareth for "The Sermon on the Mount", in which he said, "Love one another. Do good to them who persecute you."

STARTING POINT

The Way of the Clan is Love.

Albert Einstein and others have searched for a Unified Field Theory that ties in all physical phenomena.

Religions also seek to explain everything.

This writing could be called, "Tommy-Joe's Unified Field Theory", since it is a summation of my attempts from childhood to understand everything.

The realizations that an individual has about, as Douglas Adams calls it, "Life, the Universe and Everything," are truly personal.

Those realizations are most real to the individual who has them. Understanding that, I hope that in some future life, when I have once more thrust myself into ignorance, someone makes a copy of this book available to me.

LOOK FOR YOURSELF

I am not asking you to believe what I write. I would like you to look at what I write, then look to see if anything I say is real to you. Can you see, in this or any other universe, that there might be some truth in what I am writing? If you can, then you can believe me.

Ronald Reagan said, when negotiating with the Soviet Union, "Trust but verify." The most important thing you can do is look for yourself. Other people can tell you that something is bad or good, but they are always talking from their point of view and following their own agenda. That agenda may be bad or good for you. My advice, and you do not need to heed it, is to listen to others' advice, information and opinions, then check for yourself.

An example of different points of view, is my opinion of Guinness, that dark brew from St. James Gate, Dublin, Ireland, and my wife's reaction to it. We had a layover of a couple of hours in the Las Vegas airport. Our gate was just across from a bar. I ordered a Guinness. I thought it tasted great. I offered my wife a sip. She said, "That's disgusting!" Then she spit it out into her water glass. Different opinions, both valid to the person holding them, but not valid to the other person.

Karl Marx said, "Always doubt." I think that's a bit negative. "Always look," seems better to me.

Belief impairs observation. Look first, then believe all you want, but always look.

THE CLAN

The clan is the basic unit of human society. The Way of the Clan is Love.

A clan is a group of related individuals descended from a common ancestor, male or female. Civilizations come and go; empires rise and fall; but as long as women have babies, and men create a safe space for women and children, the clan remains. The Clan starts from love between a man and a woman, progresses to love between mother and child and between father and child. The clan expands outward as the generations of the clan expand. There is love between grand-parents and grand-children and between great-grand-parents and great-grand-children. The binding force in the clan Is love.

The three parts of the clan are the spirits of the clan, the bodies of the clan and the material and cultural possessions of the clan.

The spirits of the clan cycle through the generations of the clan; acquiring bodies at birth and carrying out the activities of the clan as they age; being children, having children, and as grand-parents and great-grand-parents, passing on the experience and culture of the clan to the younger generations, and when their bodies can no longer function, re-entering the cycle as the new generation.

Some of the spirits of the clan may choose not to re-enter the birth-death cycle, but to remain for a time as guardians of the clan, warning of dangers, aiding in the hunt, and generally watching over the welfare of the clan. These spirits may be honored as gods, or venerated ancestors.

In the ancient Celtic order, in Ireland and Scotland, land belonged to the four generations of the clan. The Scots who rallied to fight beside Wallace, Bruce, Graham and the Stuarts were fighting for "Scotland's King and Law", to maintain the old order.

Sadly, other Scots sought personal advantage by siding with the English. Under English law, the land belonged to the Lord, who was now able, in some cases, to clear the land of his own clansmen, to make way for the more personally profitable sheep.

Although the clan is not the official order in the so-called "developed" countries, most people still follow the way of the clan. We gather in our clans to celebrate our harvest, winter and spring festivals, births, deaths, and marriages. People with older bodies leave their possessions to their descendants. Some of the rich in America have ensured everything stays in their clan by creating foundations which own all their property. The members of the family run the foundations, but can not claim individual ownership of the things of the foundation. The individuals change, but the clan retains control.

Thomas J. Mason

THE THREE REALITIES

There are three orders or levels of reality: God, the spiritual, and the physical. God is that reality through which we are all connected and to which we are all connected. God is the source of spiritual beings, who are the source of physical universes.

In truth, the first reality is God, but from the point of view of the individual, the first reality is the fact of one's own existence.

The illusion of other is basic to being an individual. To be an individual, one must consider oneself separate from God and other individuals. Individuals choose not to know about God, to concentrate on the games they are playing as individuals. Individuals choose not to know about other individuals, to play games with them.

Close connections to other individuals enhance some games. Games in which one is defeating or harming others, require the individual to increase the separation from others to avoid experiencing the defeat or harm one is causing. To avoid excessive separation from God and other individuals, one should cause only those things that others can experience easily.

As the Golden Rule dictates, "Do unto others as you would have them do unto you." Thus one can maintain communication with others and God.

Individuals choose to reduce or increase their abilities based on the games they are playing and the roles they choose to play. Individuals allow themselves the strength they think they deserve.

The same force that drives trees to thrust upward from the ground, to raise their leaves toward the sun, runs in you, and every living thing. That same force animates the sun, moon and stars. and every particle in the physical universe.

At the level of reality that we call God, there is a oneness. There is affinity and understanding. There is no distance. Communication is instantaneous.

At the spiritual level, there are individuals. At the level of reality of the individual, there is diversity. The number of individuals is not finite. There is no limit to the number of individual beings. Each individual is unique.

At the physical level, there is existence as things. We perceive the physical universe and believe it is real, because we know that the beings mocking up the particles in it, are real. They exist, so we accept that the illusions they create exist. We are agreeing.

You are a non-mortal spiritual being.

You are a part of God.

You have created the illusion of separation to have an individual existence.

You are a part of God.

No one is closer to God than you. No one is farther from God than you. All are children of God.

You are free to be anywhere in space or time, in any universe. You are trapped or located by your decisions. You are holding in place the things that trap you. You are the source of your condition.

God is always there. We do not need to go somewhere else to be with God. We are with God now.

God created us out God's own reality to be individuals. God gave us self-determinism to get a life and go out and play.

You have an existence independent of a body or a physical universe. You are a non-mortal spiritual being who can animate a body. You take a body to have a life as that body. If you do not want to live a life as a body, the answer is simple: do not take the body.

Before you take a body, you potentially have all the abilities that holy men seek: you are outside the body; you can go anywhere you choose; you can know anything you choose. Your abilities are limited only by what you will allow.

When you take a body, your attention gets focused on the body. You are now playing the game as that body.

There are three aspects when operating a body: spirit, mind and body.

Health of the body requires health in the physical: food, water, air, environment, associates; health in the mind: removing sources of non-survival thinking, and focusing on survival and action; health in the spirit: focusing on survival of the body and all things related to that body in ever-widening circles: family, clan, tribes, nations, humans, living things, the physical environment, spiritual beings, God, ethics and aesthetics.

HIERARCHIES OF BEINGS

The idea that a body is animated by a non-material entity is common in our cultures. The Ancient Greeks believed in the trinity of "spirit, mind and body." Christians speak of the "soul". The ancient people whom we now call, "Celts", believed, and modern Hindus believe, that an individual can be reborn in another body, to live another lifetime. Hindus believe that within each body dwells a spark of the divine, the "atman", a tiny part of the Godhead, the source of all things. In his "Ender" books, the author, Orson Scott Card, uses the word, "aiua", which he took from the Sanskrit for "life", to describe non-material beings who can be pulled out of their own other-universe to animate bodies in this universe. Card speculates that they are also animating the matter in this universe.

The Hindus and Buddhists call the physical world, "the world of illusion". Others have pointed out that whatever exists is being created.

There is a hierarchy of beings creating and giving reality to the physical universe, both the "in-animate" objects and the "animated" objects that we recognize as life-forms. There is a hierarchy of beings starting with the tiniest sub-atomic particles. Above them are the beings who are being atoms, or creating the illusion of atoms. Ascending upward, we have beings who are taking responsibility for larger and larger illusions - rocks, mountains, rivers, lakes, continents, oceans, planets, solar systems, galaxies, universes. Those individuals are creating the illusion of the particles and objects and energies in this universe that we are agreeing exists. We perceive that they have their attention on something and since they are real, we believe that on which they have their attention is real. We are experiencing this particular physical universe because we are agreeing that this is what a universe should be: galaxies of stars, with planets, moons and people.

All matter, inorganic and organic, is continuously being created by spiritual beings who are being that matter, and creating the illusion of that matter for others to perceive.

The American psychic Edgar Cayce, in his reading number 3384-2, stated, "For all healing, mental or material, is attuning each atom of the body, each reflex of the brain forces, to the awareness of the divine that lies within each atom, each cell of the body."

Thomas J. Mason

OPERATING A BODY

You operate a body best from outside the body - above and behind. Good athletes do this instinctively. You have heard sports announcers saying about great athletes, comments such as, "He could see the whole field," or "He always knows where his team-mates are," or "He can see the whole ice." You can not do that from inside a head or a stomach. You need to be outside and above the body.

When operating a body from outside, it is possible to monitor it too lightly. If you wish to keep your body running, it needs food, water, air, sleep and attention.

Bodies have evolved being controlled by external spiritual beings. In addition to the seven main chakras or power centers in the body, as identified in Indian philosophy and practices, there is an eighth chakra or power center above the body that monitors and coordinates the body. External to that, and locating itself anywhere within or without the body, as it chooses, is the spiritual being who is being the "personality" of the body. That would be you. You could be considered the ninth chakra or control center of your body.

You have a choice before you take a body. You can take it or not take it.

A spiritual being is neither male of female. One can be either.

Because of past experiences, an individual may feel more comfortable being male or female. One should take a body with which one is comfortable.

Taking a body puts you in debt to the ancestors of that body. You owe it to them to continue the line of bodies into the future. Taking a body without continuing the line breaks the agreements of the clan and the expectations of the ancestors that you will provide a body for them when their time comes.

YOUR OWN RELIGION

As a child, I walked to Sunday School, then, when older, to Church, most Sundays.

At the age of twelve, I was an usher in our church, until one communion service when the choir sang the hymn, "Saved by the Blood of the Crucified One." I had a vision of stabbing someone in the side with a spear and having liquid run down my arm. The minister said, "Anyone who cannot participate in this service should leave now," so I did. Eating someone's flesh and drinking someone's blood suddenly seemed like cannibalism. Although since we were Protestants, and against the evils of drink, it was only bread and grape juice, not wine.

As a high school student, I accepted the materialist belief that Science could eventually create life in a test tube. But materialism as a philosophy failed me and I dropped out of university and got into drugs. Fortunately for me, the spiritual revival of the 1960's included a renewed interest in Eastern religions: Taoism, Buddhism and Hinduism. In an English translation of "The Song of God," as the Indian poem, "The Bhagavad Gita" is called, I read the words of the charioteer, Krishna, to the prince, Arjuna. Krishna said, "Arjuna, thou and I have lived many lives." Arjuna was filled with uncertainty before a battle. Both sides in the battle ahead of him were family. Krishna told him he must choose his actions based on what is right regardless of family. What I got out of that book was an affirmation that the spirit, the individual, is separate from the body, has lived before, will live again, and must base his actions, to the best of his ability, on what is right. In the words of Davie Crockett, "Be sure you're right, then go ahead."

What I discovered later is that separate lifetimes is an illusion, much like separate days. As a spirit, one is aware, regardless of the body going through a cycle of being awake and being asleep. One may animate different bodies, but the spirit is the same. We create the illusion of separate lifetimes so we can play the game as a new life, just as we greet each day newly after sleep.

Religion, as a set of beliefs concerning the cause, nature, and purpose of the universe, must be able to encompass all the observable data, in order to be considered valid. If it cannot explain some aspect of Life, the Universe, and Everything, especially in areas which it claims to explain, then the rest of its teachings are suspect.

A wise religion would seek only to explain those things which can be observed, and not seek to assert realities which can not be proven. The question of course becomes, whether anyone but the observer can see what the observer does. For example, from my point of view, there are three levels of reality: the physical, the spiritual and God or the divine. Yet, I have spoken to people who believe that only the physical universe exists. They have no awareness of themselves as spiritual beings, and no awareness of God.

Individuals, regardless of the religion they profess, have their own understanding of God, the spiritual and the physical, and of the relationships between them. That understanding is the individual's actual religion.

GOOD AND EVIL

Many writers and philosophers have said all is in the mind. My description of the three realities would suggest that at root, all is God. If this is the case, how can there be evil, if all is God?

That question has bedeviled saints and sinners, holy men and sages for eons. The biggest barrier to full understanding is the separation from God that allows one to exist as an individual. It is that separation that allows us to exist as individuals; to have free will; and to do good or evil.

What do I mean by "good" and "evil"? Basically it comes down to the games we spiritual beings play with each other. Good would be anything that makes the game better, more interesting, and last longer. Evil would then be anything that worsened the game, made it less interesting, and shorter.

If we use the sports analogy, good would be sportsman-like conduct and evil would be unsportsman-like conduct. Why do people engage in unsportsman-like conduct? The usual reason is fear of losing. Ear-biting in boxing, tripping in hockey, grabbing a face-mask in football, fouling in basketball, are all acts of desperation brought on by fear of losing.

People who do not "play well with others" are usually doing things that they think will benefit themselves without regard to the welfare of others. Possibly they have lost so many times they believe it necessary to harm others for them to win. Examples of this would be dictators who are willing to kill millions to remain in power, and people who feel they must lie, cheat and steal, because they cannot see any other way to get what they want.

People who "play well with others" have learned that when everyone benefits, everyone benefits, including themselves.

DO GOOD TO THEM WHO PERSECUTE YOU

Perhaps the reason I cannot walk on water, is the difficulty I have with this part of Jesus' teachings. I have always felt that those who persecuted me needed to be dealt with so they would never do it again. Oddly enough, that can be similar to Jesus' teaching. When being audited by the IRS, I found the best policy was to give them everything they wanted to prove that I really was entitled to the deductions I had taken. I'd say that policy had a ninety-nine percent success rate. Only one deduction was not approved, and that one, I had already learned, after I filed the return, was a no-go. After I provided all the documentation, I was able to continue taking the other deductions, without being audited again.

"Curiouser and curiouser," as Alice said, in Lewis Carroll's "Alice's Adventures in Wonderland". Apparently, I already follow this teaching to some extent. So there must be other, obviously minor, character faults that prevent me from duplicating Jesus's feat.

THE FUTURE

The future will be as we create it. We will come back to the world we leave to our descendants.

Nothing from our past is lost to us. Whatever we created in the past, we can create again.

The future will be as bright as we create it.

It is up to us.

Thomas J. Mason